More Praise for *Dining Al Fresco with My Dog*

Grief. Brave attitude. Small triumphs. "Dear dead
departed husband, / your being dead and departed / is
a major pain in the ass." The widow senses her husband
everywhere. Wears his shirts. Stacks the logs. Learns
to change a spark plug. Sue Fagalde Lick may make you
weep, make you smile. And then, of course, there's the
dog. This is a strong book.

—Penelope Scambly Schott, author of *On Dufur Hill*

I0089702

DINING
AL FRESCO
WITH MY DOG

DINING
AL FRESCO
WITH MY DOG

Sue Fagalde Lick

MoonPath Press

Poetry
ISBN 978-1-7348739-8-6

Cover photo, Annie photo, Author photo: Sue Fagalde Lick

Book design: Tonya Namura, using Gentium Basic

MoonPath Press, an imprint of Concrete Wolf Poetry Series, is dedicated to publishing the finest poets living in the U.S. Pacific Northwest.

MoonPath Press
c/o Concrete Wolf
PO Box 2220
Newport, OR 97365-0163

MoonPathPress@gmail.com

http://MoonPathPress.com

For Annie Mae Lick, the best dog in the whole world.

CONTENTS

DINING AL FRESCO WITH MY DOG

WHERE IS DOWNTOWN?

Midnight Hot Tub

The neighbors are sleeping, their windows dark.
Only the amber street lamp, muted by fog,
lights our way, the white-muzzled dog and I,
from house to deck to the tub that hums,
bromine feeder swirling around.

As the dog whisper-barks at raccoons,
I drop my towel and flip-flops on the chair,
push the lid open against an insistent breeze,
perch on the narrow blue plastic ledge,
and lower my restless legs into bubbly broth.

I'd only planned to soak my calves.
Lower, lower! cry my knees and thighs.
Now my robe is wet, my nightgown, too.
I fling them off. Naked, I splash in all the way
to the corner where he sat, penis afloat.

Alone in the dark, unable to see each other's eyes,
watched over by dog, trees, moon, and stars,
we'd squirt each other with little plastic ducks
and say what we kept hidden in the light until
he'd pull me close, wet breasts against his chest. . .

Bark! *No!* Mustn't wake the neighbors.
Tail up, the dog patrols the chain link fence,
then settles on the chaise lounge watching me
stick my pink-polished toes in the air,
waving at the invisible moon and stars. And him.

House Concert

Oh, I was good last night,
pounding that piano, singing like
Streisand or Joan Baez or. . .
Reba! I was all of them
there in my purple pajamas
zipping through my songbook,
changing keys, making up solos,
singing high, singing low,
imagining you listening.
Oh my God, I was good
once I took out my hearing aids.

Still Life

Nicked-up guitar
    leans against the piano
which needs tuning
    but plays all right
if you don't mind
    a few sour notes.

It's silent now,
    books on the bench,
fireplace lit at 8 a.m.,
    too dim to read notes,
the woman's fingers
    too stiff this early in the day.

On the sofa, still in her robe,
    dog warming her hip,
she recites her prayers
    for the dead and still alive.

No one sits on the loveseat
    or at the table behind her where
the one pink placemat
    has a red tomato sauce stain.

Outside, dim as twilight,
    rain pounds the hydrangeas,
fireweed fluff scatters,
    mushrooms bloom.

Kneading

Radio blasting news,
she stands at the sink
massaging Woolite
into her red sweater
as the water turns pink.

Her hands knead wool
as if it were dough
for homemade bread
that she will eat warm
dripping with butter. . .

or his stiff shoulders.
Her fingers rub, squeeze,
flatten and fold, working
in circles, pushing hard,
harder as he moans . . .

But this is just a sweater.
Rinsing away the soap,
she lifts it out, heavy,
dripping on her feet.
Her old fingers ache.

Widow's Rags

I'm dressing like a man these days.
Wore out my husband's flannel shirts,
bought some more in my own size.
I wear them over polo shirts and jeans
with lace-up leather hiking boots.
I let the girl cut my hair so short
there's nothing to grab anymore.
The back of my neck is shaved. Like his.
Sure, I have breasts, but I hide them,
and yes, I have a fuzzy face. I do.
Without my earrings and my paint,
I could pass for a man, one of those
wrinkled, rugged cowboy types.
Just slap on a Stetson hat and let
my mustache have its way.
I'm turning butch in my old age.
Now I'm wife and husband, too,
hauling the wood, cooking the steaks,
fixing the roof, driving the truck.
His clothes fit well and keep me warm.
A dress would feel foolish now,
and who is looking anyway?

Driveway Friend

He's a driveway friend, you know the kind.
When you're washing the car, he comes over,
looks around, says, "Great weather, huh?"
And you say, "Sure is" as you scrub at dead bugs
plastered to your license plate.
Maybe you mention the raccoon
that trashed your bird feeder last night,
and he says he saw a coyote here last week.
He watches you work. "Do you like venison?"
You say, "Sure." "Well, I'll bring you some."
You think about how your dog likes to lick
the crusted blood off his pickup truck
and how you hate seeing the elk head
staring from his living room wall,
and he has no idea what you do
or where you go some mornings
all dressed up with piles of books,
but you're just driveway friends
so you rinse off the bugs,
stand to stretch your aching knees
and say, "Thanks, that'll be great."
He doesn't know you don't eat meat,
but he'll forget his offer anyway.

Adventures Await

My tent took two years
and two hours to figure out.
It sat in the garage in-between.

Poles, slots, ties, stakes,
directions written for engineers
who have set up tents before.

A tent for a man who
has had adventures, who
has slept among the grizzly bears

while his wife stayed home
baking birthday cakes and knitting,
crooning to his babies at dusk.

I was the wife who stayed home,
but now that I'm left here alone,
I'm done with sweaters and cakes.

I want to go where the trail leads.
Today I set up my tent,
green and brown like the woods.

I wanted to see if I could.
Now, in my bubble of plasticized mesh,
wind breathing the walls out and in,

I kick off my shoes and open a beer.
I imagine a river nearby
where I will bathe in the morning,

dine on wild berries and fish,
sleep with the moon shining in,
grizzly bears snoring nearby.

But here, I hear the highway hum.
Dog barks at the roosters next door,
I can almost touch the chain-link fence,

my own bent and rusted fence,
neighbor mowing his lawn nearby.
But it's farther than I've gone before.

Surveillance Report

Lights go on at 6:15.
I see her in the kitchen.
Then she disappears.

7:02 at the table, gray robe,
reading, fire in the pellet stove,
dog sprawled on the loveseat.

Our records show she's 68,
widowed, no kids, alone.
She plays piano at church.

Website, blog, Facebook.
Huh. A writer. Several books.
None I'd want to read.

10:13. Still in her robe.
Standing by the stove,
writing. Cold, I guess.

12:08. Here she comes.
Dressed at last. Jeans,
baggy shirt, baseball cap.

Kitchen table. Lunch.
Dog hanging close,
she reads, eats, reads.

Now she's down the hall.
Can I take a break? There's
nothing happening here.

3 p.m. Heavy downpour,
but she's coming out.
Mismatched rain gear,

dog on leash. I'm bored.
Dog shitting. Call the cops.
Nope. She's bagging it.

6 p.m. Getting dark.
Stove, table, stove.
Sitting with the dog again.

I fell asleep. It's 10 p.m.
She takes pills, hugs dog.
Lights go out at 10:15.

End of shift report:
Eats three times a day,
keeps warm, still alive.

Smoke Signals

Across the street, gray smoke
puffs out of the chimney,
threads through spruce and alder,
and spreads out, heading west.

The kitchen lights are on,
my neighbor at the sink,
making sandwiches at dawn,
her dog alert for crumbs.

Over here, I start the fire,
turn on the kitchen lamp,
take my dog outside to pee,
put a kettle on for tea.

My smoke mingles with hers,
my lamp shines in the dark.
I look across the street and wave.
And so begins another day.

South Beach, Oregon

Where is downtown, my mother used to ask
of my patch of ground in the woods.
On 101, she'd see flashes of ocean,
an occasional house or trailer park,
storage lockers, an RV repair shop,
the seafood deli, Hoover's bar,
beach signs, and the one-runway airport
with little planes like dragonflies,
but where were the shopping malls,
churches, gas stations, and city hall?

At the postal stand, we'd stop,
say hello to Valerie, coo
at the baby on her hip,
nod to the neighbor mailing a box,
pause to scan the bulletin board.
"This is all there is, Mom."

I could see she didn't understand
as we drove down the gravel road
and turned right at the Douglas fir.
A moss-covered house, an old dog,
a circle of mother trees standing guard,
a party of robins feasting on worms—
downtown as far as I'm concerned.

Picking Berries and Dandelion Greens

As I started out for church at dusk,
I saw my neighbor limping up the road
with her white dog Harley at her side.
She carried a silver bowl of dandelion greens
snipped from the yard of the vacant house
where they started painting white on gray
and left, plastic taped over glass and doors.

I rolled down my window. "Grazing again?"
"Oh, my chickens just love this stuff
and the purple clover, too, but it's all gone.
You goin' to church?" "Yes, I am.
Choir practice on Wednesday nights."
The dog jumped at my door. "Harley, down!"
I tried to pet him but couldn't reach.

"There's tons of blackberries there," I said.
"Enough for a cobbler tomorrow night.
I plan to pick them when I get back."
"Berries, huh? Well, that sounds good.
We don't want to let 'em go to waste.
I wonder when someone's moving in."
"Dunno," I said. "Not too soon, I hope."

My car's exhaust fogged the wooded road
as the last sun tipped the evergreen trees.
"Well, you drive safe. Sing pretty."
I passed the house with the overgrown lawn.
No one was parked in the driveway yet.

Is Anyone Driving to Seal Rock?

It's dark. I can't see the stranger
in the passenger seat as I drive
through rain so hard the wipers
just sigh. I can't see the lines.

My black purse, wallet and all,
sits on the floor between us,
me and this person huddled
in a hoodie, shivering.

Though she's young, maybe 21,
she's missing her front teeth,
doesn't seem to hear me well.
Shirley, she says when I ask.

I don't pick up hitchhikers.
The seat where Shirley sits
is covered with dog fur,
gloves, the morning mail.

But it's raining like hell.
We gave her food and music.
Could I refuse her a ride
when I was going her way?

She followed me in the dark.
"Should I sit in the front?"
"Of course. Get in." I waited
as she clicked her seatbelt on.

It's like driving through a river,
blinding headlights passing by,
Shirley staring straight ahead.
"Drop me off up here," she says.

A campground south of town.
Thanking me, she tumbles out
and walks into the stormy night.
I touch my purse. Still there.

Blackjack

There he is again, the old man
whose hands break my heart,
stiff and wrinkled like my dad's.
We're nearing the end of our walk, but
he smiles. Annie speeds up,
pulls me along. He waits for us.

"Good boy," he says, patting her head.
She dog-smiles, wags her tail.
"You're a good dog, yes you are."
Finally he looks up at me.
"Lived here long?" "Twenty-two years."
"Well, I was one of the first. Name's Johnson."

Big Spruce, he calls this place.
He lives up past the iron gate.
Now, in the middle of Birch Street,
leaning on his hand-carved cane,
he pets my old girl and talks
about the dog he used to have.

"Got him up in Depoe Bay.
One day, this Dobie came running up.
'Are you mean?' I asked. Some are, you know.
He answered with a big old sloppy kiss,
sat down like he belonged. His owner said,
'Want to buy him?' I said, 'Yeah.'"

He talks like my father used to do,
words gushing out, same blue eyes
begging me to listen. I push away
thoughts of hospital beds, oxygen masks,
Dad's thin voice pleading, "Let me die."
Mr. Johnson here is still alive.

He rubs my dog's white snout.
"Oh, Blackjack was good, about this size,
best friend I ever had. His back gave out,
and I had to put him down." He stares.
A dove coos somewhere near. Wind sighs.
A white pickup passes, spreading diesel fumes.

"Well, I'm on my daily walk,
up and down this street," he says.
"Us too. Guess we'd better be going."
"I love you, boy," he tells my girl.
Tears streaming down my face,
I feel him watch us trot away.

While I Play at the Stone Soup Supper

Hear that music? See that old lady
playin' boogie on the church piano?

It's warm in here, smells like chicken,
like Grandma's house when she wasn't dead.

My own mother never cooked. Yours?
Only meth, but I hear you, bro.

What's that, some '50s music shit?
Old piano bar mama, rockin' silver hair.

Hey, I'm in line here. Wait your turn.
Don't touch my pack or I'll hurt you.

Never thought a tater could taste so fucking good.
Did you see the apple pie? Gonna get me some.

What's that song? I know it like my name.
Hey, lady? Old Joe Clark? Yeah. Thanks.

Hey dude, ask her for some hip-hop.
I hate these grandma songs.

Leave her alone. She's having fun.
I'd tip her a buck if I had one.

Shit. They're peeling up the tablecloths.
But the old gal's just hit her groove.

Where am I sleepin? Wherever.
I'm not leavin' till she quits playin'.

Tuesday Lunch at Georgie's

I'm a ripple in an ocean of tourists
come to gawk at the ocean view and eat
chowder, salmon, fish and chips,
snapping pictures to show their kids.

The waitress with the Cleopatra eyes leans close,
takes my turkey sandwich order. "Fries?" "Of course."
Today, the ocean is blue with lighter streaks
as if God were finger-painting in the waves.

A man in a plaid shirt leans against the window.
He sighs, nods, rests his head on his fist as he
listens to a city official, young with a beard,
frowns when the waitress interrupts with food.

Next to me, a woman with a scarf on her head
ignores her crab salad sandwich while her man
shovels in pasta like he's running late.
She catches me staring. I look away.

My table is brown and black laminated wood
with a dusty glass float for décor, plus
catsup, salt and pepper, sugar packets,
iced tea, mayo and mustard in little pots.

A round-faced Grandma in a baseball cap
laughs, rocking her Halloween earrings,
as she lunches with her dutiful kids
come to visit from somewhere else.

In front of me, an old man with a hearing aid
rubs an old woman's back and shoulder blades.
Neck shaven, she sits stiff. Rub, rub, rub.
I want to scream at him to stop.

A party of middle-Eastern men gather
at the big table, the only dark-skinned
customers in this gringo bistro at the beach.
Mexican busboy fills their water glasses.

A left-handed woman with wild hair writes
as she eats the pot roast special by herself
while travelers gather by the door.
Or is that me, reflected in the mirror?

This Pearl Comes with Extra Salt

We get to talking in the beauty shop,
the waitress with the dye setting in,
me under the plastic drape getting my mom hair
clipped even shorter by Karlia, whose breasts
threaten to spill out of her low-cut top,
and her little girl, on summer break, sweeping up hair
and perusing *People* magazine while the lithe masseuse
does yoga stretches beside her empty chair.

Turns out we all know Pearl, the old lady
who's everywhere and cannot be pleased.
She used to own the building where Karlia worked,
would come stomping up the stairs for rent,
squinting through the hair spray fumes,
scowling at the nail girl doing acrylic tips
on her own fingers while chatting on her phone.
Pearl hasn't changed her hair since 1942.

"Pearl!" says the waitress spinning in her chair.
"She comes to the restaurant every single day,
sits in the same booth by the window.
She doesn't like anything, I swear, even the coffee.
Too strong, she says, but she comes back every day,
and she sits there forever. Some of the girls
don't even want to wait on her. Seriously,
we fight over who gets fussy Pearl today.
But she cleans her plate, and she always tips."

In the mirror, massage girl goes into triangle pose.
"I know Pearl from church," I say. "She always
looks like she just tasted something foul."
"Uh huh," says the chorus at the beauty salon.
"I've been the victim of her tart tongue, too.
Oh yeah. She doesn't like the music, she's mad

about the candles, the chairs and the altar girl,
complains to the bishop when the priest blows his nose,
but she comes to church seven days a week."

"Then she goes to the restaurant to eat,
after which she gets a wash and set,"
says Karlia, putting her scissors down,
checking to see if my side hairs match.
When she plugs in the dryer, all I can hear is the roar
while I think about Pearl in her long wool coat,
sharing the pew with Madge, tiny, half deaf,
her lips always turned up in a smile.

"I wonder. . .does anyone know Pearl's last name,
whether she has a family, or where she lives?"
Heads shake in the silence as the dryer stops.
Karlia unsnaps the drape from around my neck.
"No, but I'm pretty sure she's kind of rich."
"And tough," says massage girl from downward dog.
"Alls I know," adds the waitress with the blonding hair,
"is I hope I'm just as strong when I get old."

"Yes!" We agree. "But nicer," adds Karlia's daughter
as she sweeps my cuttings into the dust pan
in a swirling cloud of black and gray.
The mirror shows wrinkles and perfect hair
as I write a check for thirty bucks.
I step out into the sun, thinking today
I'll invite Pearl to join me over lunch.
I know she'll probably turn me down.

Piano Man

When you hear the clunkety-clunk
on the senior center piano,
the one with hymnals stacked on top,
you know that Doug, age 94,
couldn't wait for three o'clock,
playing his Bb major songs as if this
were a honky-tonk and it was still
nineteen thirty-six or forty-two,
as if he still had teeth, his legs
didn't give like rubber, his hands
didn't hurt from *ar-thur-i-tis*.

His left hand goes back and forth,
bass-chord, bass-chord, his right
flitters loosely around the melody
until he slows to a grand finale,
leans on his four-footed cane
and proclaims, "That was nineteen-nineteen,
'Digging Flowers for My Momma's Grave.'
That's a sad one my daddy taught me."

"Anybody know that song? You don't?
What key? I don't know no keys.
I just play by ear, I always have.
I played at dances and at church,
still do. They love to hear me play."
He sits and grins as you applaud,
as if you really had been listening
instead of texting on your phone.

"Now it's your turn," he says,
rocking on the piano bench.
"Whatcha gonna sing?" You
point to the paper in your hand.

"Oh, that's a good one," he says.
It's not the version that he knows,
that he bellows loudly in your ear.
But you sit up straight and do your best
because everybody takes their turn
and Doug can't wait to play again.

Fish Tails Café

The waitress, Connie, calls me "beautiful."
I take my usual two-top near the kitchen,
sun shining on the checkered tablecloth,
under the picture of a fisherman with his halibut,
and thank her for my tall iced tea, no lemon.
I've got the menu memorized; the specials never change:

Tuna melt, turkey club, Reuben, burger, snapper,
ham and eggs, omelet, biscuits and gravy,
country fries, coleslaw, cream-of-something soup.
"Grandma, do we still have it?" Connie yells.
Younger than me, with a Southern drawl, Grandma
relays the question to José, who answers, "Sí."

The place fills with tourists and fishermen,
construction guys, couples sneaking out for lunch.
I have to shout to order the tuna melt.
I pull out my book, my journal, my phone,
and set them up like condiments
to go with the entrée when it comes.

"Here ya go, Beautiful. It looks so good."
It's just a sandwich and runny slaw,
but I set my phone and book aside
and take the bread between my lips
like I'm making love to that tuna melt,
dressing dripping down my chin.

When Fish Tails was new, I used to come
with my handsome bearded man.
No books, no phone, no journal then.
We sat at this table holding hands.
The tea and tuna melt haven't changed.
Eleven dollars, two bucks tip.

"How is it, Sweetheart?" Connie asks.
I nod, my mouth too full to speak.
I'm caught up like that halibut,
unable to resist the shiny lure
of mismatched tables, chairs that rock,
and someone who calls me *Beautiful.*

Beach Run

I awake to rain spattering the roof
and the dog licking herself. Six a.m.,
not quite light. Days getting shorter.

Down Inlet Avenue, a man, with his name
printed on his khaki shirt, drives his pickup
past as the dog squats, fur brushing wet grass.

Ocean, pewter yesterday, aquamarine today,
sky streaked gray and pale blue, we descend
the secret steps, tattered boots waffling wood.

A hidden garden path through dripping pines
and fences brings us out above the beach,
56 stair-steps down to the wet-hard sand.

The tide retreats and rolls out, crackling
over crab and mussel shells, glistening
rocks, black, white, green, and brown.

Along the water's edge, the dog strains,
pulling toward a red-jacketed woman
who returns my hoarse "Good morning."

Then the dog spots the seagulls. We run.
We fly across the sand, my heavy feet
barely touching down, gravity escaped.

At last we slow and turn, my heart
pounding, breath wheezing in my chest,
dog smiling, open-mouthed, long-tongued.

She pulls me back up to the street.
People pass on their way to work,
dressed up, holding coffee mugs.

Leisurely we sniff the flowers,
meander toward our breakfasts,
to eat kibble, toast and blackberry jam.

Bully Wind

When I heard you were coming,
I put away the patio chairs,
strapped down the garbage can,
locked the doors and hid.

But there's no getting away from you,
you who come roaring in the night,
pushing down gates, ripping the tops
off roses and early daffodils.

A rogue with no respect,
you bend and dip the spruce and pines.
Those that won't dance, you break,
flinging their branches across the yard.

You toy with the shingles on my roof,
paw at the windows, shake the doors,
rip down the wires, snuff the lights.
You leave me cold and in the dark.

You're not my first, you bully wind.
You're just cold air. I've been through worse.
He smashed my windows, broke my walls.
He made me bend and twist and dip—

Enough! Go ahead, you fickle wind.
What you break, I'll build again.
Knock me down. I'll get back up.
This little piece of earth is mine.

A Tree Falls

I was washing dishes when the tree,
a coast pine on a massive trunk,
suddenly slumped and fell
with a swish of branches and cones,
taking with it my chain link fence,
twisting my gutters like licorice.

Sponge still in my hand, I stared
at needles quivering on concrete,
fence-poles zigzagged and torn,
then rushed out to look up close,
dog sniffing at the fallen fir
as wind wrestled with my robe.

A vast swatch of sky appeared
where once was only tree,
a sky all gray and thick with rain
while the remaining pines and spruce
bowed, bent and keened in the gale,
silently shouting, *Look! She fell!*

The queen of the forest collapsed,
her trunk and branches thick and lush,
among lesser, younger trees that stood
witness with me and the yellow dog
as rain gushed out of the broken pipes
and a junco pecked at a severed limb.

Late December Interlude

We steal a brisk winter walk,
trees still dripping, leaves
turned to mud-colored mulch.

All the dogs are out, catching
this dry moment between squalls,
stopping to smell each other's pee.

Overloaded garbage bins spill
Christmas wrap and turkey pans,
Pepsi cans and flattened bows.

No more surprises in the mail,
Santa pajamas in the wash,
ham and turkey almost gone.

The air is silvery, clear and cold.
Guzzle it down, breathe it deep,
exhale everything that hurts.

Wave at every passing motorist,
even if you don't know their name.
It doesn't matter on a holiday.

As sudden thunderclouds let loose,
lift your hood and run with the dog,
tail high, ears flapping joyously.

Winter Solstice

I wake in the dark these days,
bump into furniture, stumble
over dog blankets moved in the night,

tiptoe on cold linoleum,
reaching for walls and doorways.
When I turn on a lamp, it hurts.

I open the sliding glass door,
breathe the dregs of night lit
by a waning fingernail moon.

Sunrise reaches for sunset now,
both cloaked in shades of gray,
so close they almost touch.

But wait! I think I see
the trunks of leafless trees,
a hint of color in the sky.

Midnight blue then cobalt,
royal blue then aquamarine
with fleeting streaks of pink.

My God. We've reached land,
come ashore again. The dog
barks, welcoming the day.

Tightening my robe against the chill,
I drink in the blooming colors,
remember the robin's song.

Will I Go to Heaven If I Die on
the Way to Church?

It's icy, 7:30 a.m., and my feet
can't get traction on the sidewalk,
so I tiptoe across the frozen lawn,
clear the windshield enough to see,
and ease the car down the ice rink road.
As I head downhill, I tap the brakes.
They crunch, but don't stop the car.
I slalom all the way to the highway.
Anyone coming? Can't see. Can't stop.
I spin out, fishtail, find myself
inching along a sheet of ice, chanting
"Oh God, oh God, oh God, oh God."

He ought to be listening since
I'm driving to church to play the piano
and lead the choir, if they show up,
proclaiming His glory and all, but
my hands are numb on the steering wheel,
bare fingers—no time to find my gloves—
fingers that need to hit righteous notes,
holy notes, spirit-given notes, not
flopping willy-nilly, tapping an SOS.
"Oh God, oh God, oh God, oh God."

Ice sparkles under cloudy skies,
roads perfectly glazed from edge to edge.
I steer straight between the lines,
pioneering the highway at dawn,
praying the stoplight will not turn red
before I cross the bridge into town,
see the boats, the ridged blue water,

coffee for sale on the Walgreen's sign.
Last sights for a woman sure to die.
"Oh God, oh God, oh God, oh God."

I haven't finished my will, haven't
made my bed or emptied my trash.
Who will feed my dog if I die?
It wasn't supposed to freeze today.
Staples store, crosswalks, center lane.
Slow, slow, slowly turn and toboggan
into the parking lot. Can't see
if my car is between the lines. Silence.
I clasp my trembling hands and pray.
"Oh God, oh God, oh God, oh God."

Daring Winter

Bite me, cold, with teeth of ice
that tear into my goose-pimpled flesh.

Make my skin itch and bleed. Chill my blood
till it moves like honey, and all my organs

traffic-jam, my pulse gone so adagio
I could sing a song before it beats.

Crisp my hair, redden my nose, freeze
my muscles till they barely move. You,

drifting down as winter snow,
oh, so pretty on the lawn,

just try to kill me. Go ahead,
wrap your fingers round my throat.

Squeeze. Feel your power melt away
for I am fire hot inside.

As the Gulls Laughed

Seagulls have taken over the D River Wayside
where I pause, intending to eat cold chicken and
a hard-boiled egg. (Which comes first? Well, I plan
to eat chicken, egg, chicken today.) White-breasted
gulls perch atop cars, trucks, and motorhomes,
one per roof, each king of the lot, one leg tucked,
while lesser gulls loiter on asphalt, their heads
bobbing for bugs and potato chips, defying
my steel-belted radial tires, chuckling
as I park overlooking the frothing waves,
a front-row seat at the ocean matinee.

I imagine a gull perched atop my car,
its talons ticking on the new gold paint,
ticking, ticking like the telltale heart,
like the raven that sent Poe over the edge.
No. Let others sit beneath filthy birds.
Not me. I back out, tires crunching sand.
Get out of my way, you stupid seagulls.
It's like squeezing Elvis through a mob
of fans grabbing for his hair and shirt.
At last I reach the highway's edge,
gulls filling in my tracks behind.
Fifteen minutes left to eat.

Seeking another spot for lunch, I turn
left and then turn left again
onto a winding country road, but
which road is it? I don't remember
barn, rusty cars, chain link fence.
Where was that little park by the lake,
the one near the house we almost bought,
the one with the boats and the climbing toys?
Ten minutes left, but that's okay, the park is near.

It will be peaceful, quiet, serene,
but I see no park, no roadside oasis,
just more curves and then the lake
on the wrong side of the car.

I'm heading north but needing south,
clock ticking my chicken time away,
and then it begins to rain. I see nothing
but water in my face, time gushing past.
Now I'm late. But wait. There's a road.
Back on the highway fast as a gull can fly.
I still have time to eat, but what
is that little plumber's shop ahead?
Can there be two alike, both sides of town?
The highway sign says Tillamook. No!
Trapped in traffic heading north, away
from lunch and work. Golf course,
river, pastures where black and white
cows graze in the pelting rain.

Late, too late, hungry, and I need to pee
so bad. How could I get lost in a town
with all its stoplights on one main street?
God, what a fool. I make a U-turn
in a rural left-turn-only spot and get stuck
behind a wobbly Winnebago
until I blinker at a parking lot
to stop between Bi-Mart and Sears,
cars swishing by, no ocean, no lake.
I eat one piece of chicken, no egg,
screech out of the lot onto 101,
still hungry, bladder full. I'm certain
I hear the seagulls laughing as I pass
the D River wayside park again.

Sun Drunk

January blue sky delirium
after fifty-five days of rain,
of bent-over walks in slickers,
blinded by hats and hoods,
peering through cloud-splashed glasses
as water soaks through my shoes and socks.

The roads are still wet, the puddles
dog-ankle deep, the ditches so full
we call them rivers now, but today,
this hour, the sun shines through,
lighting up nubs of daffodil shoots
and buds on the alders and blackberry vines.

The air smells like camping in summer,
like sleeping bags spread on pine needles,
pancakes cooked on the Coleman stove,
hiking with Dad to the fishing spot
(quiet so as not to scare the fish),
lake water lapping against the rocks.

The dog leads me along our winter path,
sniffing at weeds, frog slime, bones
while I stumble along, giddy on sunshine.
As the thunder clouds close in again,
sunlight pales and the air turns cold.
I just keep breathing it in and in.

Butchering the Elk

My Lab sniffs blood spots on the street,
and I know they've brought it home,
the elk my neighbors shot last night,
having hung it by its feet to bleed.

The wife, gray hair pinned up tight,
waits outside for the big green truck.
Her man will cut up the bloody kill,
and then they both will get to work.

They'll spread sheets across the living room
and over the big oak table where
they'll cut and shape the hunks of elk
into steaks, chops, sausages, and loafs.

They'll get blood all over the cozy room
where antlered heads of other kills stare
at the sofa where I have sat so innocent,
letting their big dog lick my face.

My puppy follows the trail of blood.
I tighten the leash for fear my pet will
charge the corpse like a starving wolf.
In the neighbor's shed, the chainsaw roars.

It Blows Like That

It blows like an explosion that doesn't quit,
branches flying, for-sale signs shredding,
cats landing in unfamiliar yards. It blows
like an old guy who just found out he has cancer,
so now he's throwing out his fishing poles,
not caring where they land or if they break.
It blows like one big fuck-it-all, like
air drunk off its ass, stumbling around,
knocking over drinks. It blows like a scream.
It blows like God is pissed, like
He might not stop until every sparrow,
frog, and fallen leaf is swept into space,
leaving a spinning ball of naked clay
moving gingerly around the sun.

Prisoner of War

Long ago the bulldozers came,
ripping down the pines and Sitka spruce,
tires smashing through blackberry vines,
through parsnip and tiny buttercups,
leaving a graveyard of sun-bleached trunks
among which the deer could find no food.

Now, the hard-hat men work somewhere else,
but they left their killing machine behind
in grass is so thick only a rabbit or raccoon
could mount the rusting steel hulk
to sniff at its cracking leather seat,
its gears, its knobs, a forgotten glove.

Scotch broom surrounds it like a fence,
seed pods rattling against the rails.
Thorny vines wrap around its rotting tires.
Crows perch on the top and shit
while a single purple foxglove plant
dances in front of the deadly jaws.

Scotch Broom

Never mind its reputation
for allergy-causing pollen,
its tendency to take over
every patch of ground it finds,
its upended broom shape
or the way its seed pods rattle
as the wind blows them open,
scattering plants from road to ravine.

Ignore the talk at City Hall
of forming a vigilante group
to tear the unruly intruders out,
guests that no one invited,
that fling their golden dust like laughter
and wear flowers so gaudy and bright
against the dark, sullen sky
that they melt the clouds and make it rain.

Stand in fields of Scotch Broom,
bury your face in yellow flowers,
dust your cheeks with sunshine powder,
and dance. Join the party while you can.

Cougar Bait

Nature sneaks onto my fresh-mowed lawn:
a garter snake, a newt, the shell of a robin's egg,
sometimes a rabbit nibbling dandelions.

The rabbit sees me coming out,
hears me say, "Hello, Bunny." Ears back,
it flees through the chain link, disappears.

But sometimes the wilderness gets too wild,
especially with my dog's unerring nose.
Today, she snags a severed rabbit haunch.

"Drop it! Drop it!" I yell, my voice
echoing through the neighborhood
as she lets the bloody carcass go,

fluffy fur on the black rims of her lips,
a craving for meat and skin in her eyes.
I pull her away with all my strength.

"Leave it!" I say, but I myself cannot.
She'd go looking for that haunch,
eat it bloody bones and all.

Locking the dog behind her chain link fence,
I grab vegetable bags from the kitchen drawer
and go back to find the rabbit corpse.

Lifting the haunch with the dangling foot,
so like half a chicken to be rolled in flour,
I dump it heavy into the plastic bag.

A blue eye stares up from the weeds and moss,
an earless head, an oval skull with tufts of fur.
I bury it in the woods beyond the fence.

Plastic bags in the garbage can, I wash
my hands to prep dinner, opening the fridge,
a beast of prey seeking fresh meat.

Spider Takes a Bubble Bath

Naked and nearsighted,
I step into the tub,
lower my bare bottom
toward the steaming water,
two moons suspended
so close they feel the bubbles popping.
A fat black spider scurries
sideways toward my hand.

I let go the bathtub ledge
and crash, splash,
bang my sit-bones,
create a wave so big
it sends the soap
surfing onto the floor,
soaks the pink bath mat,
and turns the room into a tiny
spider swimming pool.

The blurry black arachnid
hits a strand of water,
slides down the tile,
lands on a soap bubble,
rides it like a lily pad
toward my bare, bulbous
bubble-covered knee.
I jump out of the tub
onto the sloshing bath mat.

As I reach for a towel,
the spider climbs out,
refreshed, shakes itself,
walks straight up the wall
and out the open window
to dry off in the sun.

HOME MAINTENANCE

They Fit Like a Hug

His blue coveralls fit—if you don't heed
the crotch hanging down to my knees,
a crotch someone has mended repeatedly,
last time with purple thread, but now
the cloth is tearing away. No matter. I won't
be straining the fabric as my husband did
or pulling it open to pee standing up.

The coveralls are a marvel of cleverness,
close-woven material that won't catch
on nails, thorns, or raggedy wood,
a plethora of pockets deep and wide,
ten fat snaps instead of buttons.
I'm protected from sun, spiders, and dirt,
frayed collar to pink-painted fingernails.

They have holes in the knees, ragged cuffs,
a faded label that says Cotton 46.
A dark spot on one chest pocket hints
of a patch with a name long torn away.
Black stains on the sleeve, a dab of paint,
a smear of something reddish brown—
I can only add to the history of these coveralls.

As I slip them over my shorts and shirt,
snap by snap, he seals me into the arms
of this well-worn armor that hid in the closet
next to his robe and his good blue suit.
Taking up his clippers and leather gloves,
I head out to battle the blackberry vine
just beyond the chain link fence.

First Time

I've become obsessed with lawn-
grass, veldt, sward,
pasture, plain, prairie, llano—
green blades that must be cut
before they grow so tall
my socks and shoes get wet,
the bumblebees get lost,
and the dog takes a bath
by rolling in the morning dew.

I once had a gardening man.
He'd arrive with his army of tools,
a roaring battalion of steel
that left the lawn with a GI cut
from house to fence and along the sides.
I would inhale the fresh-sliced scent
while the dog ran joyful curlicues
and robins came to hunt for worms.

But the gardening man has gone away.
The lawnmower from another life
has rusted in the backyard shed.
Sure it won't work, I pull it out,
feed it gas and oil and yank the cord.
It roars to life, dragging me
into fences and walls, ravenous
for grass, dirt, and dandelions.

It mows a labyrinth into the green,
a maze that ends in no escape,
I fight to turn it into rows.
It's like trying to trying to stop a pickup truck
with nothing but my little hands.
Sweating, sore, about to weep,

I collapse into the new-mowed grass.
It prickles my neck and arms.
I can feel it growing under me.

If I Were a Guy

I wouldn't be so wussy about the lawnmower.
I'd straddle that monster, pull its cord
and tell it where to go.

I'd mow down daisies and dandelions,
give that overgrown lawn a soldier cut
and make that green grass fly.

I'd throw off my shirt and bronze my skin,
muscle up my delts like a man
and reek of cigarettes and sweat.

I'd weed-eat my way through the yard,
wielding my trimmer like a sword,
cutting every live thing in its path.

I'd crank up the blower good and loud,
headphones blasting my favorite tunes,
blow everything out of my way.

I'd sling my gear up into my truck,
wink at the old lady writing the check
who wishes she was ripped like me,

and I'd ride my Ford like a stallion,
feel it rough between my legs,
and look for another lawn to mow.

Up High

Don't climb the ladder alone,
my dad would say. *You'll fall*

and die or fracture your skull.
Women don't belong up there.

I ignore his voice as I
set my feet on the bottom step.

The ladder shakes. I see it fall,
feel the sidewalk breaking me.

But that won't get the gutters
clean, so I step up and up

till I can see across the roof
into the neighbors' yard. I wave

at the German shepherd watching me.
Don't worry, Dad, I'm holding on

as I reach into the mud and guck
and watch it splatter on the lawn.

Painting the Shed

Snatches of song play in your head,
the Name Game—*paint, paint, bo-baint,*
banana fana fo faint. John Lennon singing
"Shake it up baby now, twist and shout,"
then "Porgy, I's your woman now, I is, I is. . ."
Even last Sunday's gospel acclamation
spills out of your cluttered brain
as you bend, dip your brush into the bucket,
and slap on the blue-gray paint,
learning the wood like you never did before.

The eaves are two by fours, two smooth sides,
one rough that won't take in the blue.
Between them, the underside of the shingled
roof is ragged, as if nibbled by raccoons.
The west-side boards, 18 of them, are scarred
by sideways rain and wind chimes knocking them
in a frenzy of winter song. On the east, sheltered
by fence and trees, the boards are smooth but furred
with orange algae and tufts of clinging green moss.
As you paint, branches poke at your spattered arms,
tip your baseball cap. Spiders scurry from your brush.

The front, 15 boards around the new white door,
pitted by hail and blasting sun, drinks in paint
and wants more, leaving white spots to patch
tomorrow when you paint the back, squeezing
between the tarped woodpile and the wall.
Where you can't reach, you use a roller on a pole.
The paint sprays your face, gets in your teeth
as you shout and groan, reaching, reaching, arms
screaming, *Enough!* but there's that one spot. . .

Paint on your nose, your lips, your cheeks,
streaked and splattered on your red sweats,
your ruined first-job tee shirt, your arms,
spilled on the grass and dirt below the shed.
Dog watching from the deck, you step back,
set down your empty bucket and brush
and sink onto the lawn with a sigh. Done.

Stacking Wood

The neighbor man shoved wood from the fallen pine
through the splitter, an orange machine on wheels
that he drove with his truck across my lawn.

Rain soaking his bald head and flannel shirt,
he forced fat circles of tree against the six-inch blade
and ripped them apart with his leather-gloved hands.

He tossed the wood onto a pile, its milky innards
exposed, bark coming off like potato peels,
sawdust browning the grass and dandelions.

Me, I stood on my lawn and watched,
old widow worried about her grass
and her dog eyeing the open gate.

He left tire tracks and that mountain of wood.
That night after supper, I put on my gloves
and the sweatshirt I'd ruined with paint.

The wood-rack was rusty, the tarp was torn,
my bones likewise wearing away. Spiders
circled my yellow tennis shoes.

Bend, lift, place the logs on the rack.
Round edges, flat edges, bits sticking out,
branches I could neither break nor bend.

One row, then another, then a third,
higher and higher, yet the pile seemed
never to shrink. Oh my back, my back.

The dog darted in, grabbed chunks of wood
in her mouth, crunched them into kindling,
white pieces left shredded and sharp.

Bend, pick up the jagged logs, hold them snug
against my shirt, ignore the dirt, wedge them
in among the other ones. Bend again. My back!

The stack was nearly as tall as me when
I pulled the tattered tarp across the top,
praying the mountain wouldn't avalanche.

Bark, dirt, leaves, tiny bits of wood
swept into the compost cart for garbage day,
I removed my gloves and rubbed my back.

I gazed into the ruddy sunset sky.
Let winter come. Let it rain and snow.
The wood will burn. The grass will grow.

A Moment

Sweaty from wrestling with overgrown
blackberries, ferns, and miscellaneous weeds,
counting the bites on my summer-bare arms,
I sprawl under the just-trimmed alder tree,
pleased at how its branches sprang up,
suddenly light as the dead weight fell.

Spread-eagled, the yellow dog and I
ride our piece of moss-covered earth,
softly panting, cooled by the sweet grass,
robin feeding among the dandelions,
butterfly gliding up, down, and around,
savoring its joyful moment of being alive.

I am old, but lying here under
yellow-green leaves backlit
against the cloudless sky,
warm dog at my fingertips,
I feel light as the alder tree,
rooted here for eternity.

Your Widow Reporting In

Dear dead departed husband,
your being dead and departed
is a major pain in the ass.
Like today when the mail
brought me a big juicy check
issued in your name only,
but you're a dead guy with no
bank account while I'm here
hugging the dog for warmth
because the six thousand dollar
boondoggle of a radiator
doesn't work and I'm waiting
for this kid named Kevin
to order a part, a switch meant
to keep the house from burning down,
and yes, I got this house from you,
but it's too big and stuff keeps
breaking. Not that I don't try.

I can change a spark plug now,
cut branches with a pole saw,
light a hell of a woodstove fire,
and I'm getting the bills all paid
somehow, but I haven't figured out
how to eat without a book to read—
and not to eat your share, too—
nor I can puzzle out any way
not to flinch when I see couples
hugging or holding hands. Sweetheart,
I so loved your scabby fingers,
and now you don't have hands at all.
You're just ashes in a brass urn
that I visit to change the flowers.
Gold for autumn, red for Christmas,

a little flag for Veterans' Day,
as if you give a damn. Yes,
it's all a pain in the ass,
a heater sitting dead and cold,
a check I'll never get to spend,
a hand I'll never get to hold.
But I'm tough. I'm getting by.
I just thought you'd want to know.

If Superman Came to My House

I wouldn't ask him to save me
from some evil villain with a knife or gun
or scoop me bleeding off the floor.
All that stuff's just fantasy.
No. I'd have him fix the sticking door,
de-moss the roof and patch the leaks,
unclog the sink, repair the stove,
and remove the rats beneath the house.
Now that would be a super man,
not some guy in tights and greasy hair
who thinks I'm helpless, 'cause I'm not.
I just need another set of super hands.

Morning Service

At six a.m. when it's still dark
and you wish you had more sleep,
but you've cleaned your plate of dreams
and, besides, the dog wants out,
you feel the top of the pellet stove
like taking a child's temperature.
Cold. Rolling up your bathrobe sleeve,
you kneel and open the tabernacle door,
feeling in the pot for clinkers.
Slate-hard down in the ash,
they tear at your fingertips.

When all is clean, you shut the door,
wipe your hands on a torn-up towel,
nudge the thermostat to sixty-eight,
watch sparks dance like fireflies.
Pins and needles in your feet,
you stand beside the dog and pray
for a hint of sun between the clouds,
then reluctantly turn on the lights.

Recipe for My Home

Take dish towels from my hope chest,
pots from my wedding shower,
pictures from my hippie honeymoon,
the poncho I crocheted in college,
a bookshelf from my grandpa's house,
along with his dusty accordion,
Grandma's recipe for Shepherd's Pie,
the rings from my second marriage,
a cabinet from my mother-in-law,
a stack of Mom's piano music,
my father's faded flannel shirt,
my husband's Giants baseball cap.
Mix all these things from other lives.
Stir in today's mail, an old guitar,
purple hydrangeas from the yard,
Red Zinger tea in a Hawaii mug,
blueberry muffins and a grapefruit half,
an open book, page thirty-five,
and a dog gnawing on a rawhide stick.
Form into a loaf and let it rise.

Mandolina

Autumn sun on the Oregon coast.
A house among the spruce and pine.
A fresh-stained redwood deck.

An old woman in flannel and jeans
plays a beat-up mandolin with stubby
paint-stained fingernails.
She stamps the beat with her tennis shoe,
hears the whole band in her head.

"Redwing," "Liberty," "Old Joe Clark,"
she single-notes, double-stops,
chunks chords on 2 and 4,
singing verses in her crackled voice
that used to be so clear and sweet,

but it doesn't matter now. The band
disbanded long ago. The half-deaf dog
sleeping among the dandelions
is her only audience, but she still dreams

of someone, anyone, standing at the gate,
harmonizing, clapping, coming in to jam.
But outside the rusty chain link,
she sees the same old trees, the neighbor's
purple car that hasn't run for years,
the propane tank that's running low.

Fingers sore, she sighs, adjusts her cap,
listens to the robin singing in the alder tree
and the waves roaring in, swishing out.
She counts the beat and starts again.

Dining Al Fresco

"Do you want to eat inside or out?"
As soon as I say the words,
I hear my mother asking my dad
the same question, circa 1963.
In the summer in San Jose,
100 degrees in the house,
the answer was usually yes.

At his decree, we sprang into action.
As the daughter, it was my job
to carry everything out
on a tarnished silver tray.
Back and forth, kitchen to patio,
two steps down, two steps up,
I juggled cups and lemonade,
plastic tablecloth, four plates,
paper napkins folded in half,
silverware to hold them down.

Dad, freshly showered after work,
tended the smoky barbecue,
sipping Miller's from a can.
My brother, I don't know,
playing some game in his room,
not in training to be a mom.

Back and forth, down and up,
potato salad, big yellow bowl,
chili in the smaller green,
olives in the smallest, red.
Ketchup, sliced white bread,
butter on a plastic plate.

When the meat was done,
he'd ring the bell. Aprons off,

Mom and I brought the rest.
We straddled the wooden benches
that flanked the redwood table,
my little brother next to Mom,
who passed the bowls around.

As we ate, our father recounted his day
building houses in post-war suburbia:
Oakies, Dagos, the foreman, the kid,
wires, ladders, pipes, and *two-by-fours,*
goddamn this, *bullshit* that.
As he swatted flies, I saw the fresh cuts,
the blackened thumbnail failing off.

Squirrels chirped in the walnut tree.
Robins pulled worms from the lawn.
A breeze cooled the sweat on our necks
as we reached for more of everything.
Food just tasted better outside—
and we had chocolate cake for dessert.

Now as I ask "inside or out?"
already knowing what I prefer,
the silent dog just watches me
go back and forth, up and down,
one fork, one plate, one glass of wine
on a placemat on a TV tray.

I set her bowl down on the deck
as the robin hops across the grass
and raccoons prowl beyond the fence.
Bless us, O Lord, and these thy gifts. . .
I wish we'd said Grace or thank you
to Mom, Dad, or God just once.
I wish I'd saved that silver tray.

Reunion

When I come home, she pins me down
and sniffs me all over, checking.
Have I hugged another dog today?
Have I eaten a cookie, leaving crumbs
embedded in the pink yarn of my sweater?
Have I walked in the woods untethered
by the leash, without her along
to protect me from wild rabbits
and dogs that might lead me astray?

I sit still, feeling the breath
puffing from her leathery nose
against my cheeks, my arms, my neck,
until finally she sighs,
stretches long against my leg
and rolls slowly over on her back
so I can run my fingers from
her naked belly to her chest
and bury my nose in her tweedy fur,
inhaling the places she has been.

Dry Bones

Within earshot of the crowded beach,
we crunch along the hot gravel road—
yellow grass, deer shit, smashed snakes,
just-turned blackberries gray with dust.

I urge the dog toward the fruit, but,
head thrust into salal and Scotch broom,
she's chasing a bit of bread, a banana peel,
a not-quite-empty Starbuck's cup.

Here, a fisherman dumped his leavings,
crab shells, halibut guts, spiny skeletons
stinking in the sun, for the dog to snatch
while I holler, "Drop it, drop it, drop it!"

Half deaf, she doesn't hear a blue pickup
roaring toward us, churning up a cloud.
The driver waves, his mutts straining
to join the rotten seafood feed.

Sweatshirt tied around my waist,
phone banging against my hip,
my legs ache, but we need to move,
our old bones as dry and brittle

as the fish spines and berry vines
baking to dust in the August sun,
leaving a plastic Starbucks cup
rolling downhill toward the sea.

Power Play

Hood over baseball cap,
I can only see straight ahead.
Rain so hard the drops on my coat
merge into solid wet.
My jeans cling to my thighs.
I'm cold, but the dog
leashed to my left hand
meanders, sashays, saunters,
pulls me left and right.
She sniffs every dot of shit,
licks every wrapper or cup,
chews the weeds like licorice.

"Let's go," I whine.
She gazes up at me, plants
her paws on the pavement
as if to say, "Make me."
She's dry inside her fur,
eighty pounds of will.
It's like trying to move a bus
with a skinny nylon strap.
As cars swish by, I wait,
water seeping through my shoes.

Holding Air

"Peace be with you.
And with your spirit.
Let us offer each other
a sign of peace."

The hand holding mine
during the Lord's Prayer,
that raised mine high
at the end, lets go.

I am left holding air
while on either side,
kids high five, couples kiss
or shake their babies' hands.

In a minute or so,
they'll remember me
for a hasty handshake
as we begin to sing

"Lamb of God, have mercy
on us, Lamb of God,
have mercy on us, Lamb
of God, grant us peace."

Poppies

When the gardeners came, they murdered my poppies,
seeing them as weeds to be eradicated by the blade
that edged the lawn and tore away the ivy considered
an evil invasive plant. I liked my poppies,
grateful for every orange flower that volunteered
to grow where roses and azaleas wouldn't take.

    Ancestry.com says my people were poppies, too.
    Maria from Baja raised 13 kids and ended up,
    old as I am now, working as a maid, scrubbing floors,
    a poppy in an orchid house. Anna, widowed young,
    cleaned the church, cut cots, took charity
    to feed her seven Portuguese-speaking kids.

They cut the wild blackberries, too, as if
I weren't planning to bake blackberry crumble,
muffins, pie, and coffeecake, not too proud
to compete with the robins to pick my share,
even from a branch lying on the ground.

    Louisa tended the bread in the wood-fired stove,
    tossed grain to the chickens, collected eggs,
    fired her shotgun to scare the crows away
    while Paulina made schnitzel and apple pie,
    her apron stained and wearing thin.

With their chainsaws, they trimmed the alder tree,
cut back the laurels, the Sitka Spruce. They mowed away
the dandelions and clover with the lawn as I watched,
mourning from the kitchen sink, my flowers lying
lifeless as they blew the autumn leaves away.

    Mary from the Azores lost her fisherman,
    wed a man who worked in a Gloucester cotton mill.

Their son, a foreman at a California cannery,
married Anna's daughter Anne. From them came
my mother Elaine, and from her came me.

The gardeners drive away. Silence.
On dirt-stained shoes, I venture out
to survey the damage. Berries down.
Raw edges of amputated pines. But ah,
one poppy still waves gaily in the wind.

Here, surrounded by my mother trees,
robins feeding on the crewcut lawn,
I write the story that ends with me,
the last poppy, wide open to the sun,
blackberry crumble almost done.

ACKNOWLEDGMENTS & GRATITUDE

The author thanks and gratefully acknowledges the publications in which the following poems were published previously:

"Dry Bones," *Better Than Starbucks*, Feb. 2021

"Is Anyone Driving to Seal Rock?" *Windfall*, Fall 2020

"Picking Blackberries and Dandelion Greens," *Cirque*, Spring 2022

"Smoke Signals," *Willawaw Journal*, March 2018

"South Beach, Oregon," *Cirque*, Fall 2023

"Widow's Rags," *Willawaw*, March 2018

ABOUT THE AUTHOR

Sue Fagalde Lick has long lived a life that doesn't fit
the mainstream script for women of her generation.
Married twice, divorced once, widowed once, she never
had children. At 44, she escaped life as a journalist in
Silicon Valley with her late husband to live out their
dreams on the Oregon coast. She earned her MFA in
creative writing at Antioch University Los Angeles at
51 and has birthed more than a dozen books, including
fiction, nonfiction, and poetry, while building a second
career as a musician. While others her age devote their
days to grandchildren and volunteer work, she writes,
teaches, talks, walks, and sings her own song.

Her poems have appeared recently in numerous literary
magazines and the anthologies *From Pandemic to
Protest, Opening the Gate,* and *Into the Azorean Sea.*
She has published three chapbooks: *Gravel Road Ahead,
The Widow at the Piano,* and *Blue Chip Stamp Guitar.*
Her prose books include *Stories Grandma Never Told*:
*Portuguese Women in California, Azorean Dreams,
Childless by Marriage,* the novels *Up Beaver Creek* and
Seal Rock Sound, and the forthcoming memoir *No Way*

Out of This: Loving a Partner with Alzheimer's. When not writing, she leads an alternate life as a Catholic music minister.

Visit Sue Fagalde Lick's blogs at www.childlessbymarriage.com and www.unleashedinoregon.com and her website at www.suelick.com.

www.ingramcontent.com/pod-product-compliance
Lightning Source LLC
Chambersburg PA
CBHW031132020426
42333CB00012B/337